YOUR PASSPORT TO CHILE

by Golriz Golkar

CAPSTONE PRESS
a capstone imprint

Published by Capstone Press, an imprint of Capstone
1710 Roe Crest Drive, North Mankato, Minnesota 56003
capstonepub.com

Copyright © 2025 by Capstone. All rights reserved. No part of this publication may be reproduced in whole or in part, or stored in a retrieval system, or transmitted in any form or by any means, electronic, mechanical, photocopying, recording, or otherwise, without written permission of the publisher.

Library of Congress Cataloging-in-Publication Data is available on the Library of Congress website.
ISBN: 9781669087205 (hardcover)
ISBN: 9781669087151 (paperback)
ISBN: 9781669087168 (ebook PDF)

Summary: What is it like to live in or visit Chile? What makes Chile's culture unique? Explore the geography, traditions, and daily lives of Chileans.

Editorial Credits
Editor: Carrie Sheely; Designer: Elyse White; Media Researcher: Jo Miller; Production Specialist: Tori Abraham

Image Credits
Alamy: Album, 12, christopher Pillitz, 21, Eric Gohl, 5, Jon G. Fuller/VWPics, 8, The Picture Art Collection, 11, Krys Bailey, 9; Getty Images: Alex Reyes, 27, julio donoso, 13, mathess, 22, Print Conllector, 10; Shutterstock: abriendomundo, 16, Cacio Murilo, 6, Carlos D Pavletic, 17 (bottom), Coni_Munoz, 14, Diego Grandi, 19 (middle), 20, Dmitry Pichugin, 18, Dudarev Mikhail, cover (bottom), Foto 4440, 19 (top), Gil C, cover (flag), Guaxinim, 17 (top), Jeremy Richards, 25, ribeiroantonio, 19 (bottom), stas11, cover (map outline), Sun_Shine, 15; SuperStock: John Warburton Lee, 29

Design Elements
Getty Images: Yevhenii Dubinko; Shutterstock, Flipser, Net Vector, pingebat

Any additional websites and resources referenced in this book are not maintained, authorized, or sponsored by Capstone. All product and company names are trademarks™ or registered® trademarks of their respective holders.

CONTENTS

CHAPTER ONE
WELCOME TO CHILE! 4

CHAPTER TWO
HISTORY OF CHILE 8

CHAPTER THREE
EXPLORE CHILE 14

CHAPTER FOUR
DAILY LIFE 20

CHAPTER FIVE
HOLIDAYS AND CELEBRATIONS 24

CHAPTER SIX
SPORTS AND RECREATION 26

GLOSSARY 30
READ MORE 31
INTERNET SITES 31
INDEX 32

Words in **bold** are in the glossary.

CHAPTER ONE

WELCOME TO CHILE!

The sun sets over the Atacama Desert in northern Chile. The dry desert stretches far and wide. The sky is red and orange. Soon, countless stars will appear in the sky. In the morning, **geysers** will shoot up in the air. During the day, llamas will roam the desert. Flamingos will bathe in the desert's **lagoons**. Chile is a land of many wonders, old and new.

A LONG AND NARROW COUNTRY

Chile lies on the western coast of South America. The sandy coastline runs more than 4,000 miles (6,437 kilometers) long. The country is very narrow. Its average width is 110 miles (177 km). The north has dry deserts. Lakes, forests, and snowy **volcanoes** are in the south. **Fertile** farmland lies in Chile's central region. Three mountain ranges run through the country. The Andes Mountains run along Chile's eastern border with Argentina.

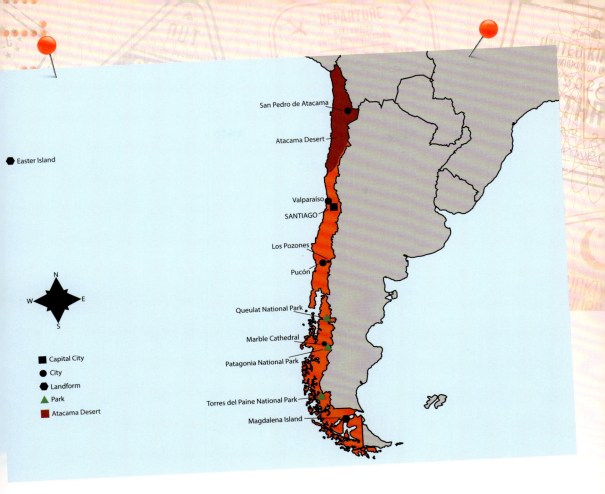

The climate varies throughout Chile. The north has a dry climate with little rain. The central region has cool winters and warm summers. The south is cold and windy.

FACT

Chile is a country with one of the largest number of volcanoes. It has about 2,000.

THE CHILEAN PEOPLE

More than 18 million people live in Chile. Almost all Chileans have mixed European and **Indigenous** backgrounds. Others have only Indigenous backgrounds. Most Indigenous people are from the Mapuche group.

Many people live, work, and shop in Santiago.

FACT FILE

OFFICIAL NAME: REPUBLIC OF CHILE
POPULATION: 18,549,457
LAND AREA: 287,187 SQ. MI. (743,812 SQ KM)
CAPITAL: SANTIAGO
MONEY: CHILEAN PESO
GOVERNMENT: PRESIDENTIAL REPUBLIC
LANGUAGE: SPANISH
GEOGRAPHY: Chile is bordered by Peru and Bolivia to the north, Argentina to the east, and the Pacific Ocean to the west.
NATURAL RESOURCES: copper, lithium, grapes, apples, potatoes

The languages of Chile reflect the country's different **cultures**. Spanish is the official language of Chile. Most people speak it, including Indigenous groups. But Indigenous people also speak their own languages. The Mapuche language, Mapudungun, is the most common Indigenous language spoken in Chile.

CHAPTER TWO
HISTORY OF CHILE

Nomads who traveled from place to place first lived on the land that is modern-day Chile. They arrived around 15,000 BCE. By 8000 BCE, hunter-gatherers were living there. They hunted animals and gathered fruits.

Indigenous people lived in the region by 600 BCE. These groups adapted to their surroundings. Some hunted and fished. Others grew crops. Some groups made ceramics, pottery, and leather crafts using materials they found.

A museum in Chile has ceramic pottery made by the Tiwanaku. This civilization lived in Chile from about 500 to 1000 CE.

In the 1400s CE, the Inca empire expanded south to modern-day Chile. The Inca ruled over the area for nearly 100 years. During this time, Indigenous people remained on the land. The Inca ruled over the Indigenous people and forced them to pay taxes. Many Indigenous groups adopted some Inca traditions. But other groups, such as the Mapuche, refused to listen to Inca rulers or change their ways. They fought the Inca in battles. The Mapuche successfully stopped Inca expansion into their territory during the Battle of the Maule. The Mapuche kept their land and traditions.

Remains of an ancient village called Tulor stand in the Atacama Desert.

SPANISH RULE

Around 1536, Spanish conquerors arrived. They took over parts of South America, including Chile. Many Inca were killed during warfare or after getting diseases. The Kingdom of Chile became a Spanish territory in 1541. Indigenous people fought the Spanish for nearly 400 years. Once again, the Mapuche were the most successful.

Over time, the Spanish mixed with the local Chilean population. More people had mixed Indigenous and European backgrounds.

The Mapuche became skilled horseback riders.

Chile officially declared its independence on February 12, 1818.

INDEPENDENCE

In the early 1800s, Chilean citizens fought Spain for independence. In 1818, the Chileans won. But there were disagreements on how to run the new country. Leaders changed often. Over time, the country modernized. Railroads were built. A university was created. Trade and mining made Chile wealthier. Large groups of European settlers arrived.

INDIGENOUS PEOPLE OF CHILE

At least 500,000 Indigenous people of different groups were living in Chile when the Spanish arrived. Some, such as the Picunche and the Huilliche, were eventually defeated. Many were forced to work in mines and fields. But the Mapuche persisted. They now live in settlements in southern Chile.

BUILDING A MODERN CHILE

From 1879 to 1883, Chile fought Peru and Bolivia. Chile won the war. It took over parts of those countries. But Chileans had problems within their country. Many thought the wealthy had too much power. New political parties formed. They represented the middle and lower classes. Many workers in mines, factories, and transportation spoke up. They wanted better pay and working conditions. But they still struggled to get what they wanted.

In May 1879, a Peruvian ship sank the Chilean ship *Esmeralda*.

From 1891 to 1973, government leaders changed many times. Augusto Pinochet took over Chile in 1973 as a **dictator**.

In 1990, Patricio Aylwin Azócar became president. He was elected by the Chilean people. Poverty rates dropped, and people earned more money.

TIMELINE OF CHILEAN HISTORY

ABOUT 15,000 BCE: The first nomads arrive on the land of modern-day Chile.

8000 BCE: Hunter-gatherers arrive.

600 BCE: Indigenous groups live in the region.

1400s CE: The Inca empire expands to include Chile.

1536: Spanish conquerors arrive in South America. They take over countries including Chile.

1541: The Spanish establish the Kingdom of Chile as their new territory.

1818: Chile becomes an independent country.

1884: A treaty is signed to end fighting between Chile and Peru in the War of the Pacific. Chile gets more land.

LATE 1800s: A wave of European immigrants arrives, and mining becomes a major industry.

1904: After the War of the Pacific, Chile officially gets control of the Bolivian coast after a treaty is signed.

1925: A new constitution increases presidential powers and separates church and state.

1970: Salvador Allende becomes the president of Chile.

1973: Allende is removed from office, and Pinochet rules Chile as a dictator.

1990: Patricio Aylwin Azócar becomes the president of Chile.

2022: Gabriel Boric becomes the president of Chile.

Patricio Aylwin Azócar (right) served as president until 1994.

CHAPTER THREE

EXPLORE CHILE

Chile offers both modern cities and abundant nature areas. Traveling across the country takes people through changing landscapes.

MODERN CITIES

Santiago is the capital of Chile. Visitors can see the historic Plaza de Armas square. They can enjoy the mural street art that shows Chile's history. Visitors can learn about historical art at the Museum of Pre-Columbian Art. A walk, cable car, or **funicular** ride up Santa Lucia Hill or San Cristóbal Hill offers a sweeping city view. Visitors can ride elevators up the Costanera Center to overlook the city too.

People ride cable cars up San Cristóbal Hill.

Valparaíso is a lively port town. The city is known for its art galleries, murals, and building designs. People can walk along beaches. Funiculars carry people to the city's many vibrant neighborhoods. Visitors can go to the La Sebastiana Museum. It was once home to the famous Chilean poet, Pablo Neruda.

The unique four-story La Sebastiana Museum was named a National Historic Monument.

FACT

An earthquake destroyed much of Valparaíso in 1906. It killed more than 3,000 people.

AN ANCIENT ISLAND

Easter Island is one of the most **remote** inhabited islands in the world. Polynesians settled the island. They called it Rapa Nui. Its landscape includes grasslands, volcanoes, and white, sandy beaches. The population is about half Chilean with a European background and half Indigenous people. The island has more than 900 giant stone carved statues called moai. The moai were carved between about 1100 and 1650 CE.

Moai stand along a shore of Easter Island.

NATURAL WONDERS

Chile has many beautiful natural areas. Los Pozones is a group of seven hot springs near the town of Pucón. People relax in the warm waters and enjoy views of the Villarrica volcano.

The Marble Cathedral is found in Lake General Carrera. This cave system formed more than 6,000 years ago. The marble caves sparkle blue from the reflection of the water. Visitors sail through the area on small boats.

A hanging **glacier** is located in the **rain forests** of Queulat National Park. It hangs from a rocky cliff. A waterfall pours out of it into an icy lake below.

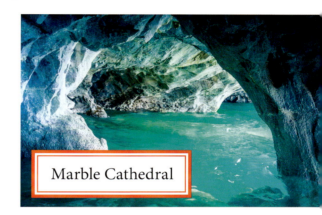

Marble Cathedral

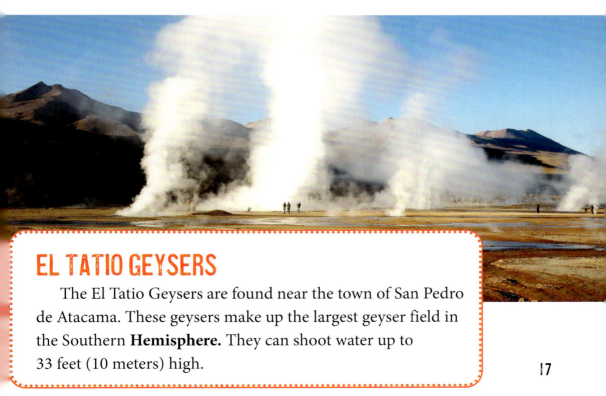

EL TATIO GEYSERS

The El Tatio Geysers are found near the town of San Pedro de Atacama. These geysers make up the largest geyser field in the Southern **Hemisphere.** They can shoot water up to 33 feet (10 meters) high.

NATIONAL PARKS

Chile has more than 40 national parks. Patagonia National Park has many animals, including armadillos and cougars. Guanacos also live in the park. These animals are related to llamas. They eat many of the park's plants.

Torres del Paine National Park has three large granite **summits**. The park is full of lakes and glaciers. Bird-watching is popular there. Andean condors, Chilean flamingos, and Magellanic woodpeckers make their homes in the park.

Guanacos

Vicente Pérez Rosales National Park features waterfalls over turquoise lake waters. Native small mammals such as lesser grisons roam the land. Birds called coots can be found in ponds. About half of all animals in Chile are endemic to the country. This means that they are found only in Chile. The country has the largest percentage of endemic animals in the world.

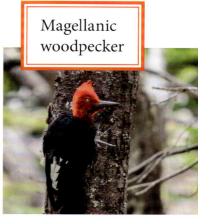

Magellanic woodpecker

Lesser grison

AMAZING GLACIERS

Chile is home to nearly 80 percent of all glaciers in South America. The El Morado Glacier melts into a lagoon. It helps nearby rivers keep their flow during droughts. The San Rafael Glacier is more than 30,000 years old. It is one of the country's largest glaciers.

CHAPTER FOUR
DAILY LIFE

Most Chileans live in cities. Buses, cars, and trains provide transportation. City residents often work in service jobs. They may work in tourism or transportation. Some work in the forestry or mining industries. Others work in factories.

Some people who live in rural areas are farmers. They grow grapes, apples, tomatoes, and potatoes.

Some Mapuche live in rural areas in wooden homes. They build these homes with hay roofs. Many Indigenous people are farmers. Some are pastoralists who raise livestock and move with the animals.

Busy streets in Santiago are a common sight.

CLOTHING

Chileans usually wear modern clothing. For celebrations, some people wear traditional clothing. The Chilean cowboy, or huaso, style features a poncho and a straw hat. Women may wear a huasa dress for a special dance called the cueca.

Mapuche have their own colorful traditional clothing. Their ponchos often have a crisscross pattern called the guemil. It is a symbol of their culture.

A musician dressed in a traditional Mapuche poncho

21

FOOD AND DRINK

Chilean food is rich and flavorful. Breakfast is often bread and jam with milk or coffee. Lunch is the main meal. It may feature meat with rice and vegetables. The national dish is cazuela. This stew is made with meat and vegetables such as pumpkin, corn, and potatoes. Seafood dishes include eel stew with vegetables and spices. Dinner is often a light, one-dish meal. Common desserts include puddings and custards. Cakes and cookies are enjoyed on special occasions.

Street market foods include empanadas. They are crunchy dough pockets with meat and vegetable fillings. Pumpkin fritters and potato pancakes are also popular.

Cazuela

CHILEAN COCADAS

Chilean cocadas are sweet, crunchy cookies served at birthday celebrations or on holidays. You will need an adult to help you make them.

Ingredients:
- 4 cups shredded, sweetened coconut
- ¾ cup sweetened condensed milk
- 2 ½ tablespoons cornstarch
- 1 teaspoon almond extract
- 1 teaspoon vanilla extract
- ¼ cup powdered sugar

Directions:
1. Preheat oven to 400°F.
2. In a medium-sized bowl, mix the coconut, milk, cornstarch, almond extract, and vanilla extract. Make sure the ingredients are mixed well.
3. Let the mixture rest for five minutes.
4. Use a tablespoon to gently scoop up a spoonful of batter at a time. Drop each spoonful onto a cookie sheet covered with parchment paper. Make sure to space the cookies about 1 inch (2.5 centimeters) apart.
5. Bake the cookies for 15 to 20 minutes. They are ready when they are light golden brown.
6. Remove the cookies from the oven and let them cool.
7. Use a sifter to lightly dust the cookies with powdered sugar. Enjoy!

CHAPTER FIVE
HOLIDAYS AND CELEBRATIONS

About six out of 10 Chileans are Roman Catholic. These Chileans and others who follow Christian religions celebrate Christmas. On Christmas Eve, families eat a large barbecue dinner. They also enjoy a special fruit cake. They go to church and sing carols. Children receive presents.

Independence Day is celebrated on September 18. Sometimes it is celebrated for a week. Chileans dance and have barbecues in parks. Horse races and greased pole climbing contests are held. Cities have fun parades.

Many Indigenous groups follow their own ancestral calendar. They celebrate the new year on the winter **solstice**. The Mapuche celebration is popular in southern Chile. The Mapuche give thanks for the harvest. People dance, share stories, and eat traditional foods.

Cueca dancers perform in a parade celebrating Independence Day.

The Tapati Festival on Easter Island takes place in February. People paint their bodies with symbols of their culture. People sing, dance, and tell stories. Some compete in swimming and canoeing races. A festival queen is crowned at the end of the event.

FACT

During Independence Day celebrations, cities all over Chile hold giant fairs called fondas. People set up large, decorated tents in public places such as parks.

CHAPTER SIX

SPORTS AND RECREATION

Chileans enjoy many sports. Soccer is a favorite national sport. Many Chileans watch professional teams play. The men's and women's national teams have played in the World Cup.

Chile's geography is also perfect for water and snow sports. Some people enjoy swimming. Diving, kayaking, surfing, and kitesurfing are popular. Winter sports include skiing and snowboarding. Hiking in parks is also common.

FACT

Goalkeeper Christiane Endler was a star player on the women's national soccer team for many years.

Thousands of people gather in large stadiums to watch soccer matches in Chile.

RAYUELA

Rayuela is an old game from rural Chile. It is also played during some national festivals.

1. Fill a plastic box or tub that is about 40 by 40 inches (102 by 102 cm) with sand or dirt. Stretch a long piece of string across the box or tub.
2. Each player will have a small rock or disc to throw. Players choose a spot from which each person will stand and throw the rock or disc. There can be as many players as you wish.
3. The first player throws their object toward the string in the box. The player must try to land the object closest to the string.
4. The next player takes a turn. Each player takes a turn to complete one round.
5. The player whose object falls closest to the string wins.

The National Rodeo Championship takes place in Rancagua each year.

RODEOS

Chileans also watch and play traditional sports. The Chilean rodeo has been popular for more than 400 years. Two people ride on horses in a big arena. They try to catch a calf with a lasso. Rodeo season begins in September and runs through April. A national championship is held at the season's end.

A UNIQUE COUNTRY

Chile is a country of natural beauty and beloved traditions. From exploring parks and cities to celebrating holidays, Chileans are proud to embrace their homeland and culture.

GLOSSARY

culture (KUHL-chuhr)
a people's way of life, ideas, art, customs, and traditions

dictator (DIK-tay-tuhr)
someone who has complete control of a country, often ruling it unjustly

fertile (FUHR-tuhl)
good for growing crops; fertile soil has many nutrients

funicular (fyu-NI-kyu-lur)
a cable railway going up a mountain

geyser (GYE-zur)
an underground spring that shoots hot water and steam through a hole in the ground

glacier (GLAY-shur)
a large, slow-moving sheet of ice

hemisphere (HEM-uhss-fihr)
one half of Earth

Indigenous (in-DI-juh-nuhs)
a way to describe the first people who lived in a certain area

lagoon (luh-GOON)
a shallow pool of seawater separated from the sea by a narrow strip of land

rain forest (RAYN FOR-ist)
a thick forest or jungle where at least 100 inches (254 cm) of rain falls every year

remote (ri-MOHT)
far away, isolated, or distant

solstice (SOL-stiss)
the days of the year when the sun rises at its northernmost and southernmost points

summit (SUHM-it)
the highest point of a mountain

volcano (vol-KAY-noh)
a mountain with vents through which molten lava, ash, and gas may erupt

READ MORE

Bowman, Chris. *Chile*. Minneapolis: Bellwether Media, 2020.

Gagliardi, Sue. *Easter Island*. Mendota Heights, MN: Apex Editions, 2023.

Vourvoulias, Sabrina. *Nuestra América: 30 Inspiring Latinas/Latinos Who Have Shaped the United States*. Philadelphia: Running Press Kids, 2020.

INTERNET SITES

The History of Easter Island for Kids
bedtimehistorystories.com/the-history-of-easter-island-for-kids

Kiddle: Chile Facts for Kids
kids.kiddle.co/Mapuche

National Geographic Kids: Chile
kids.nationalgeographic.com/geography/countries/article/chile

INDEX

animals, 4, 8, 18, 19, 20, 29

Bolivia, 7, 12, 13

Easter Island, 16, 25
El Tatio Geysers, 17

foods, 20, 22, 23, 24
funiculars, 14, 15

glaciers, 17, 18, 19

Inca, 9, 10, 13

Independence Day, 24, 25
Indigenous people, 6, 7, 8, 9, 10, 11, 13, 16, 20, 21, 24
Mapuche, 6, 7, 9, 10, 11, 20, 21, 24

Los Pozones, 16

parks, 17, 18, 19, 24, 25, 26, 29

Patricio Aylwin Azócar, 12
Peru, 7, 12, 13
Pucón, 16

rodeos, 29

Santiago, 6, 14, 20
soccer, 26, 27
Spanish people, 10, 11, 13

Valparaíso, 15

ABOUT THE AUTHOR

Golriz Golkar is the author of more than 70 books for children. Inspired by her work as an elementary school teacher, she loves to write the kinds of books that children are excited to read. Golriz holds a B.A. in American literature and culture from UCLA and a master's degree in education from the Harvard Graduate School of Education. Golriz lives in France with her husband and young daughter, and they all love reading together.

SELECT BOOKS IN THIS SERIES

YOUR PASSPORT TO AUSTRALIA
YOUR PASSPORT TO BRAZIL
YOUR PASSPORT TO CUBA
YOUR PASSPORT TO EGYPT
YOUR PASSPORT TO ENGLAND
YOUR PASSPORT TO GERMANY
YOUR PASSPORT TO JAPAN
YOUR PASSPORT TO MEXICO
YOUR PASSPORT TO PORTUGAL
YOUR PASSPORT TO SAUDI ARABIA